Smith

INSIDE ANIMALS

Written and Illustrated by

Gale Cooper, M.D.

A Mad Hatter Book
Slawson Communications, Inc.
San Diego

© 1987 Gale Cooper
Illustrations © 1987 Gale Cooper

Published in 1987 by Mad Hatter Books, Slawson Communications, Inc.,
3719 Sixth Avenue, San Diego, CA 92103-4316
First published in 1978 by Atlantic–Little, Brown Books
First published in Great Britain in 1981 by Hodder & Stoughton Ltd.

The drawings of the guinea pig are modeled after the author's illustrations in *The Anatomy
of the Guinea Pig*, by Gale Cooper, M.D., and Alan L. Schiller, M.D., published in 1975
by Harvard University Press.

Library of Congress Cataloging in Publication Data

Cooper, Gale.
  Inside animals.

  Originally published: Boston : Little, Brown,
© 1978.
  "A Mad Hatter book."
  Includes index.
  Summary: Introduces some rather unique aspects of
many different animals such as: an earthworm has both
male and female reproductive organs, a camel's hump
stores fat, and a snake has one lung.
  1. Anatomy, Comparative — Juvenile literature.
2. Zoology — Miscellanea — Juvenile literature.
[1. Animals — Miscellanea] I. Title.
QL806.5.C66 1987   591.4   87-4526

ISBN 0-915391-23-6

Printed in the U.S.A.
91 90 89 88 87 10 9 8 7 6 5 4 3 2 1

To the animals of the world
and
With love to Rudy Vaca and thanks to Irene Weiss,
Emilie McLeod, Julian Donahue, Mary Havlichek, and
Albert Morse

CONTENTS

Much understanding of how animals behave and how their bodies work comes from looking inside them. All the parts, both inside and outside, which make up an animal are called its anatomy. Separate parts that do special jobs are called organs. For example, a stomach is an organ since it helps to collect and digest food. An eye and an ear are also organs.

In this book we will first look at a single cell. Then we will learn about several different animals. Finally we will see many different examples of how special parts of special animals help them carry on their lives.

ANIMAL CELL

Every part of every animal is made up of tiny structures called cells. Although the cells of a body cannot live on their own, they can nevertheless eat, get rid of wastes, and reproduce.

To look at a cell you need to use a microscope.

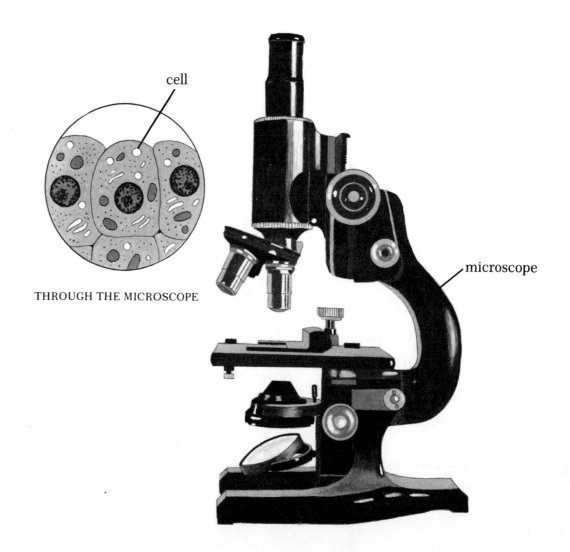

cell

THROUGH THE MICROSCOPE

microscope

This is a close-up of a cell. It could be part of an organ belonging to you, to an elephant, or even to a mouse.

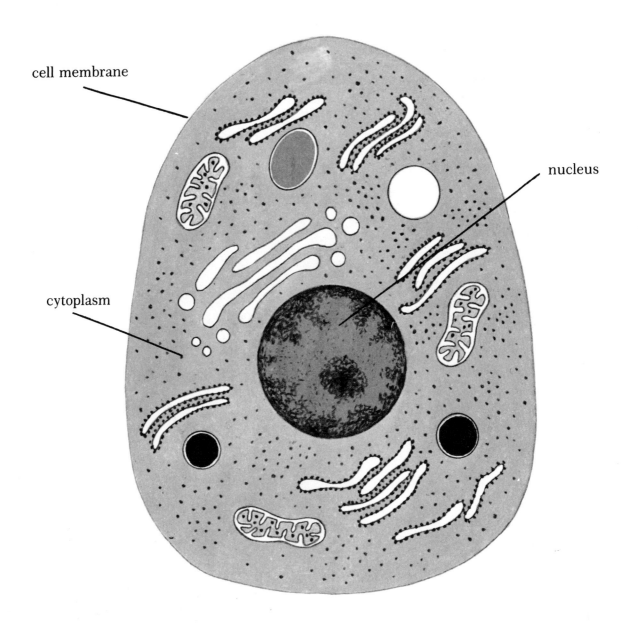

cell membrane

nucleus

cytoplasm

AMOEBA

Some animals are just one cell big. Without a microscope they look like this . . .

An amoeba is made of a single cell. It
lives in ponds and eats plants and animals
even smaller than itself.

This is how an amoeba eats.

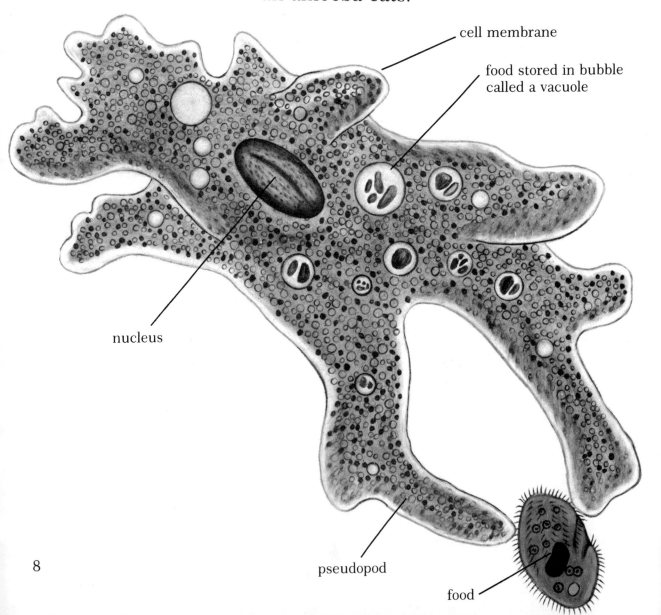

cell membrane

food stored in bubble
called a vacuole

nucleus

pseudopod

food

PARAMECIUM

Another one-celled animal is the paramecium. Even though it is so little, it has all the parts it needs to carry on the life functions of eating, eliminating wastes, and reproducing.

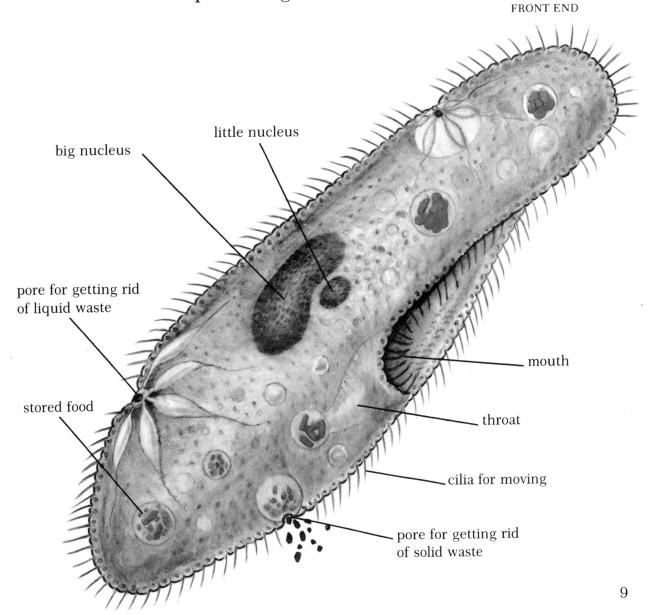

FRONT END

little nucleus

big nucleus

pore for getting rid of liquid waste

stored food

mouth

throat

cilia for moving

pore for getting rid of solid waste

9

CLAM

The clam is made of many cells. It lives in a shell which it makes itself. Inside the shell are its many organs.

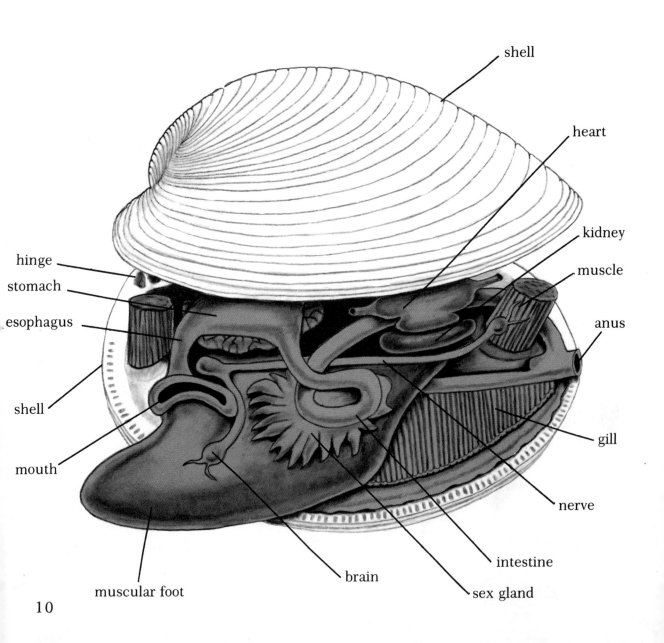

shell

heart

kidney

muscle

anus

gill

nerve

intestine

sex gland

brain

muscular foot

mouth

shell

esophagus

stomach

hinge

EARTHWORM

No matter what the shape of an animal, all the organs fit inside.

The earthworm has both male organs and female organs.

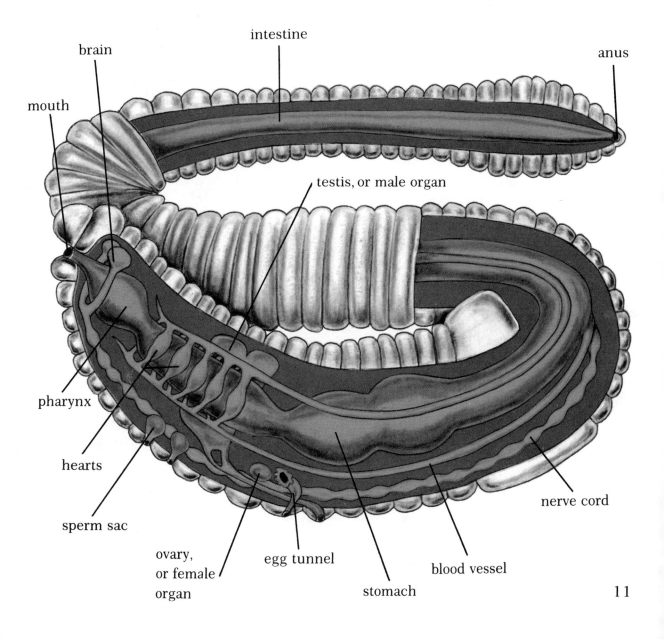

intestine

brain

anus

mouth

testis, or male organ

pharynx

hearts

sperm sac

nerve cord

ovary, or female organ

egg tunnel

stomach

blood vessel

11

STARFISH

The starfish does not have a right side or a left side. Its arms are arranged like spokes on a wheel and it can move in any direction. Look underneath a starfish and you see thousands of tiny suction feet.

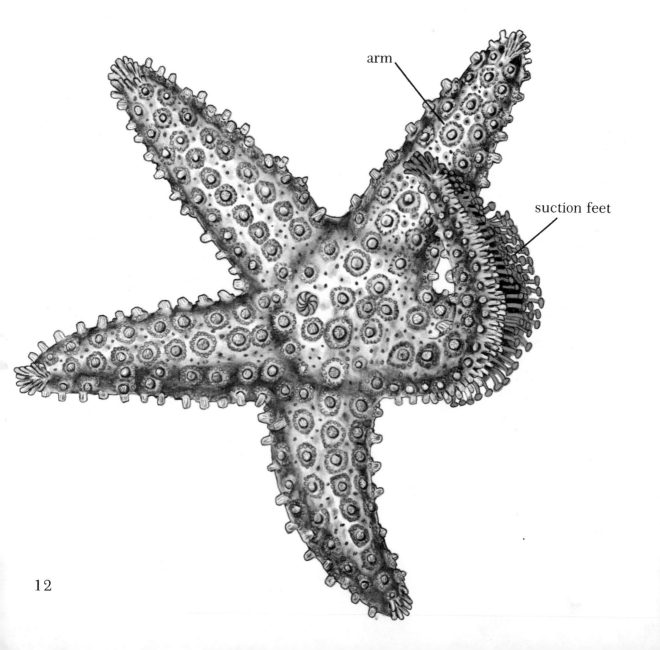

arm

suction feet

CRAYFISH

Crayfish have a very stiff shell which protects their many soft organs.

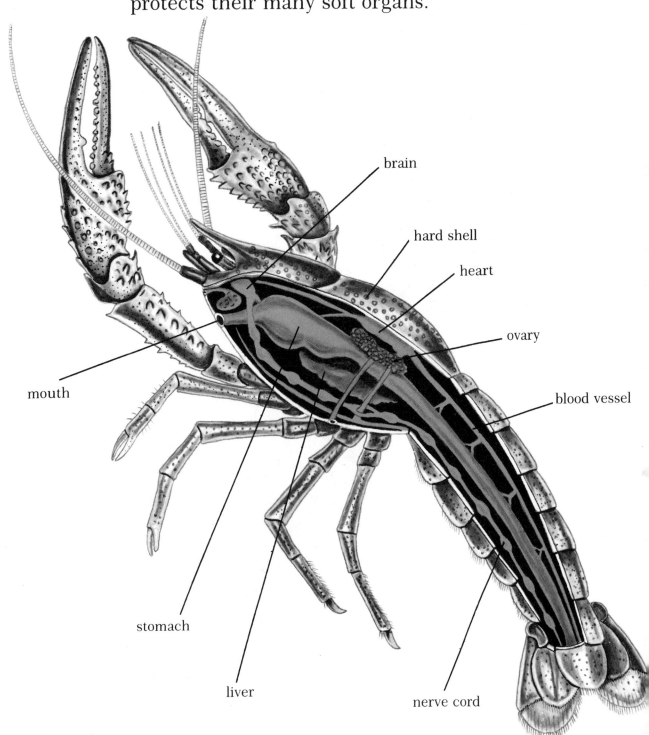

GRASSHOPPER

A grasshopper is hard outside and soft inside like a crayfish. It does not have lungs. It breathes through holes on its sides instead of through lungs. Air is carried along tiny channels or tubes through its body.

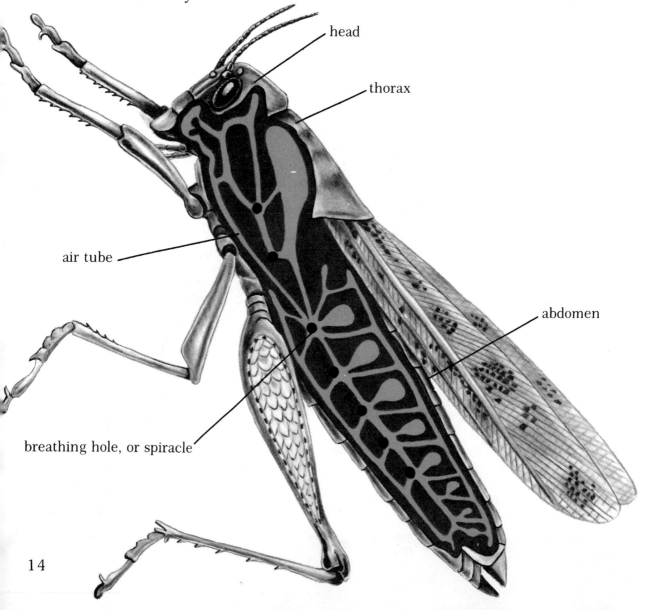

head

thorax

air tube

abdomen

breathing hole, or spiracle

Here are the rest of its organs.

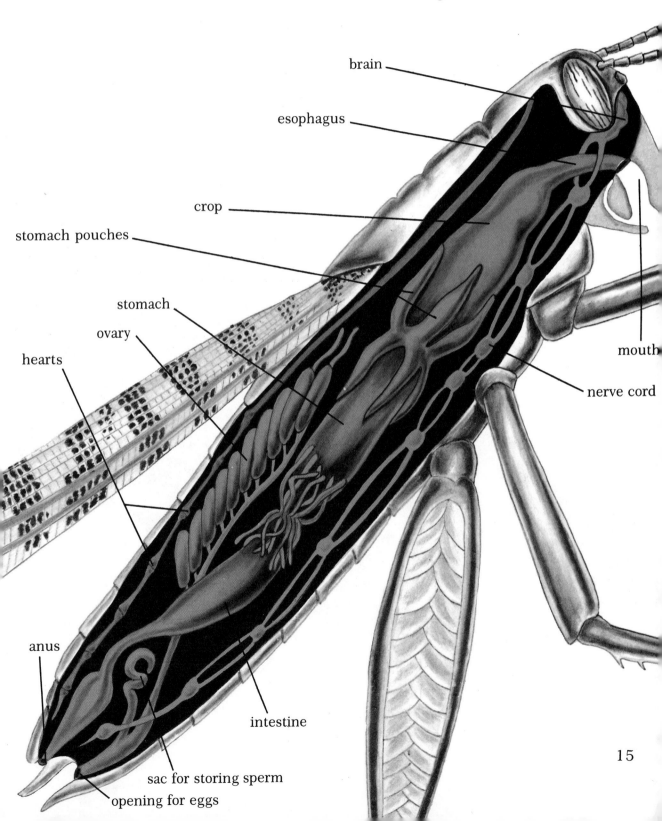

brain

esophagus

crop

stomach pouches

stomach

ovary

hearts

mouth

nerve cord

anus

intestine

sac for storing sperm

opening for eggs

15

SHARK

A shark is a fish with large jaws and sharp teeth. It breathes through gills and has the same organs other animals have.

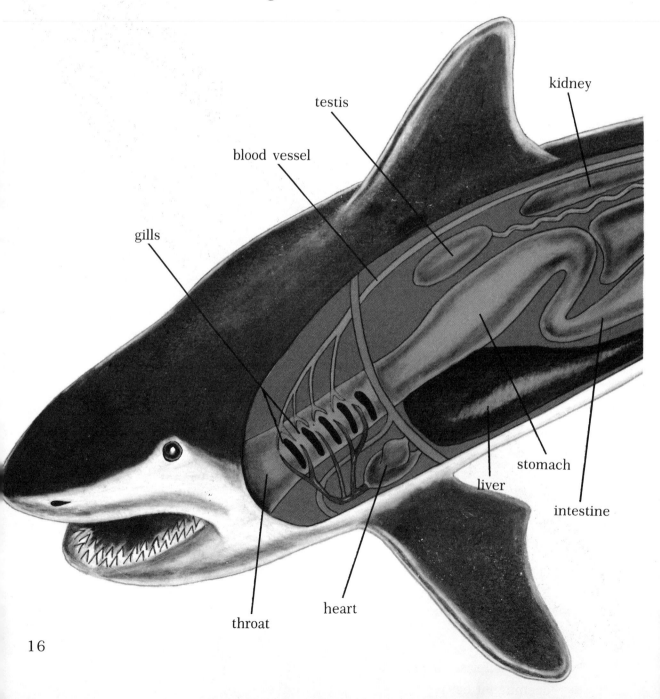

testis

kidney

blood vessel

gills

stomach

liver

intestine

throat

heart

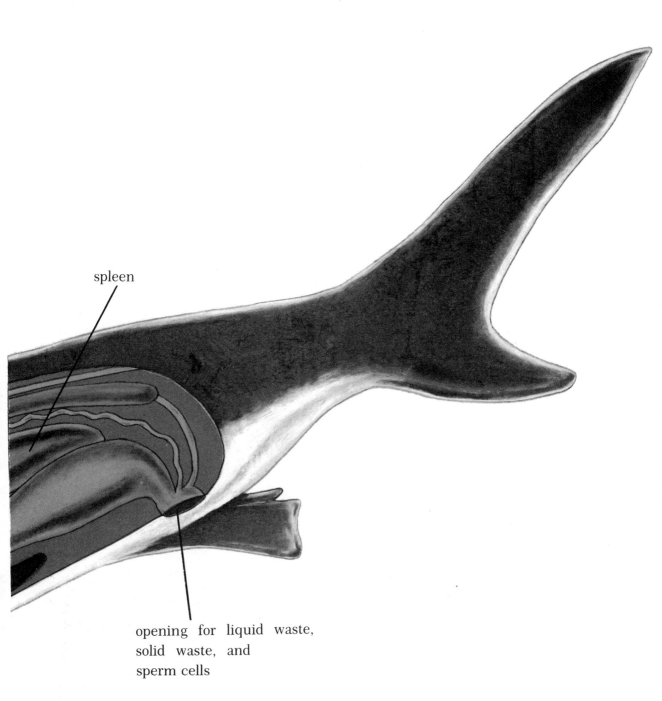

spleen

opening for liquid waste,
solid waste, and
sperm cells

PERCH

One little fish, a perch, can teach us a great deal about how all fish live in water.

It has gills to filter oxygen out of the water and to get rid of the carbon dioxide waste.

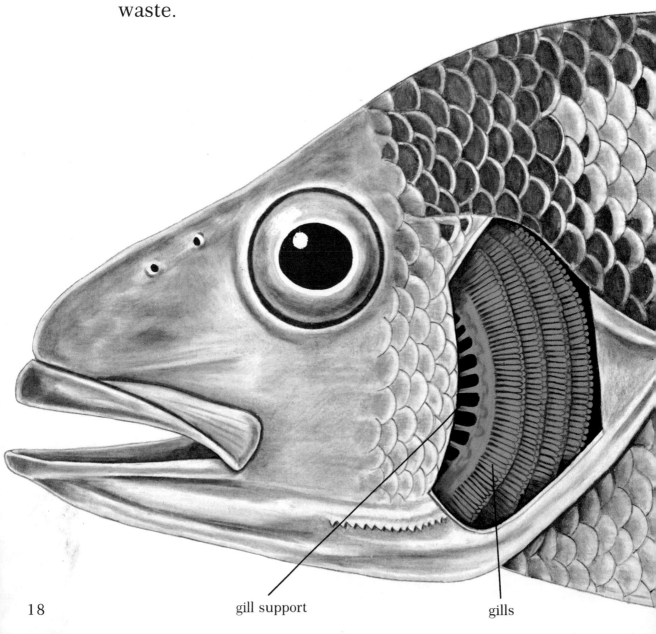

gill support   gills

Inside the perch is the skeleton that supports it, the muscles that move it, and organs that carry on life functions.

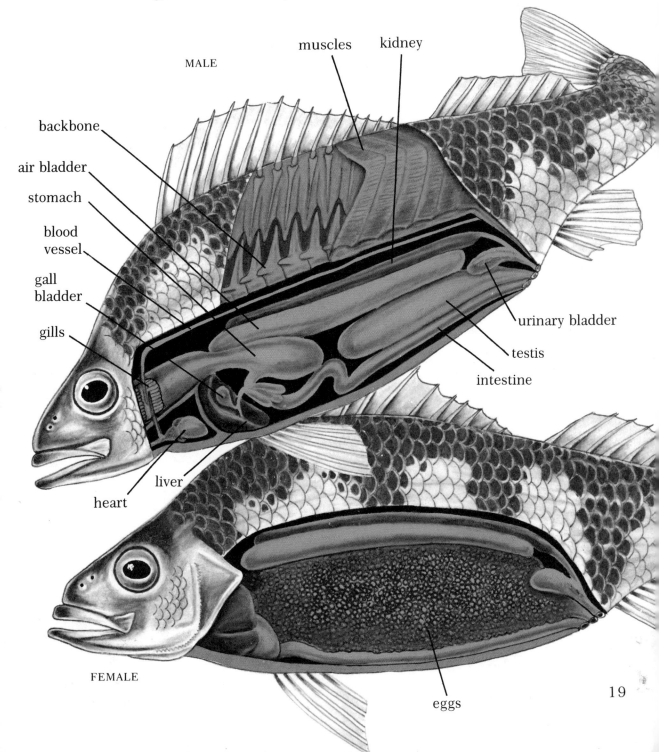

MALE

muscles

kidney

backbone

air bladder

stomach

blood vessel

gall bladder

gills

urinary bladder

testis

intestine

liver

heart

FEMALE

eggs

19

FROG

The frog is an amphibian. This word means that it can live both on the land and in the water.

When a frog is a baby, or tadpole, it lives underwater, eats plants, and breathes with gills. When it grows up, it lives on land and in water, eats worms and insects, and breathes with lungs.

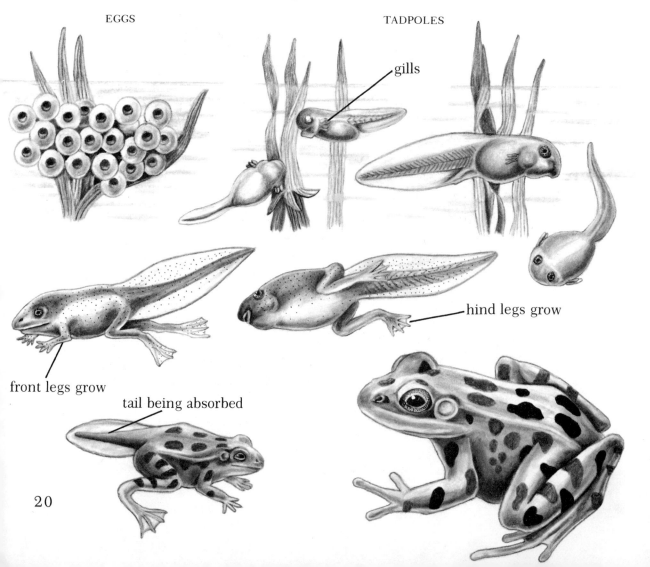

EGGS

TADPOLES

gills

hind legs grow

front legs grow

tail being absorbed

20

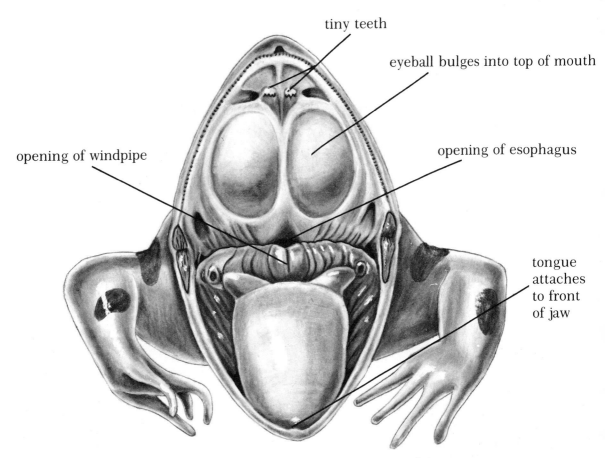

tiny teeth

eyeball bulges into top of mouth

opening of windpipe

opening of esophagus

tongue attaches to front of jaw

Looking inside the mouth of a frog helps us understand how it catches food and eats. A long, sticky tongue lies on the bottom of the mouth. The frog catches a fly with its tongue, flicks tongue and fly into the mouth, and grips the fly with two tiny teeth. The frog's eyeballs bulge down into the top of its mouth. The frog swallows by pushing the food down toward its throat with its eyeballs. That is why a frog blinks every time it swallows.

Outside of a Frog

The outside of a frog is covered with moist skin. The frog can breathe through its skin as well as through its lungs.

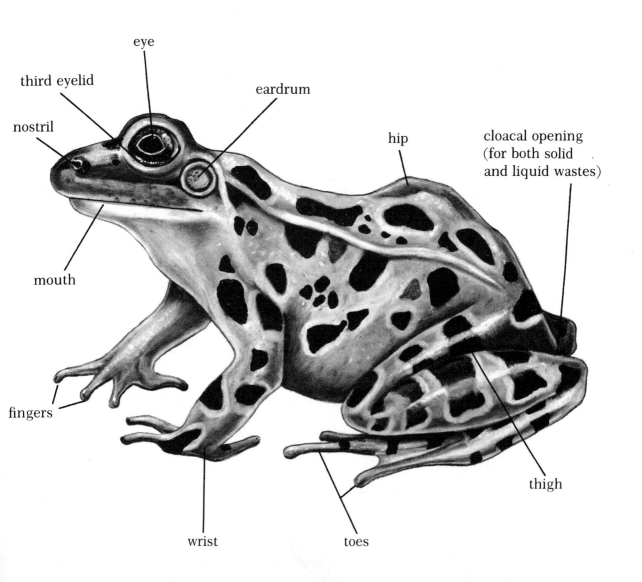

Muscles of a Frog

The muscles are under the skin and are attached to the bones.

gastrocnemius muscle
for jumping

Skeleton of a Frog

The bones make up the skeleton which supports the body.

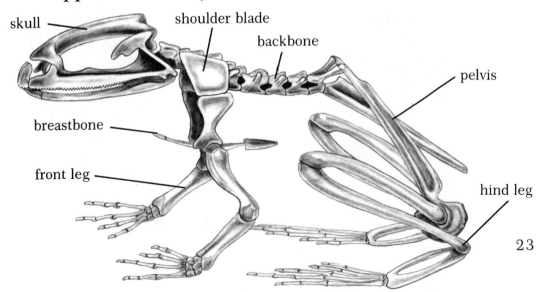

skull

shoulder blade

backbone

pelvis

breastbone

front leg

hind leg

23

Inside the Body Cavity of a Frog

The careful cutting of skin and muscle to
look inside an animal is called dissection.

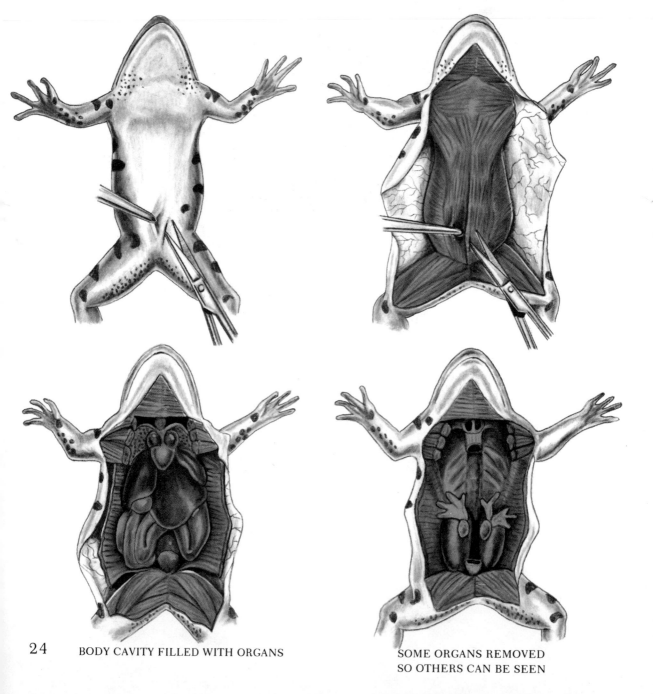

SKINNING

CUTTING THROUGH MUSCLES

BODY CAVITY FILLED WITH ORGANS

SOME ORGANS REMOVED
SO OTHERS CAN BE SEEN

Organs of a Male Frog

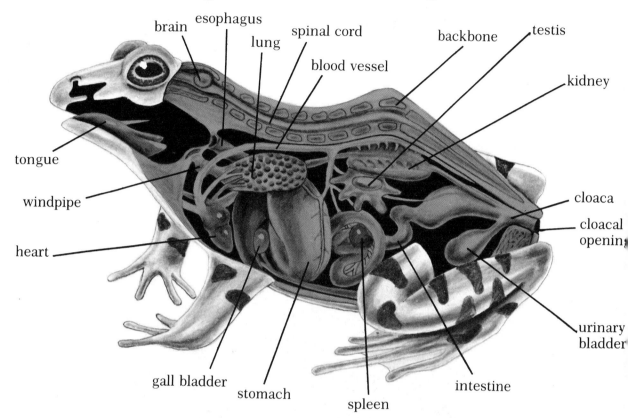

brain · esophagus · lung · spinal cord · blood vessel · backbone · testis · kidney · tongue · windpipe · heart · cloaca · cloacal opening · urinary bladder · gall bladder · stomach · spleen · intestine

Organs of a Female Frog

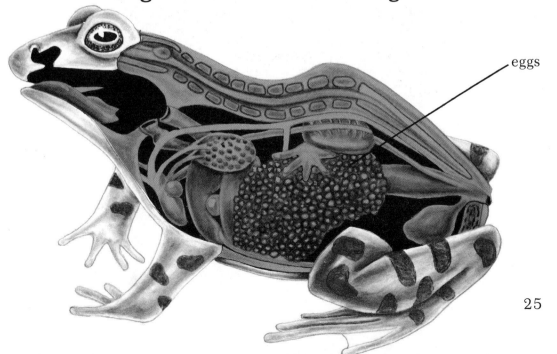

eggs

Looking More Closely at the Organs of an Adult Frog

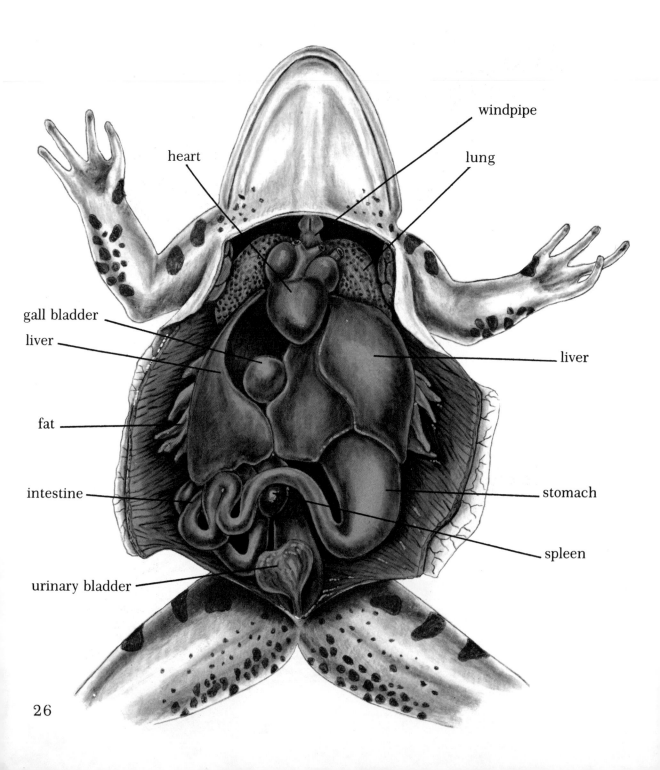

windpipe

heart

lung

gall bladder

liver

liver

fat

intestine

stomach

spleen

urinary bladder

A tadpole looks very different from the adult frog, inside as well as outside.

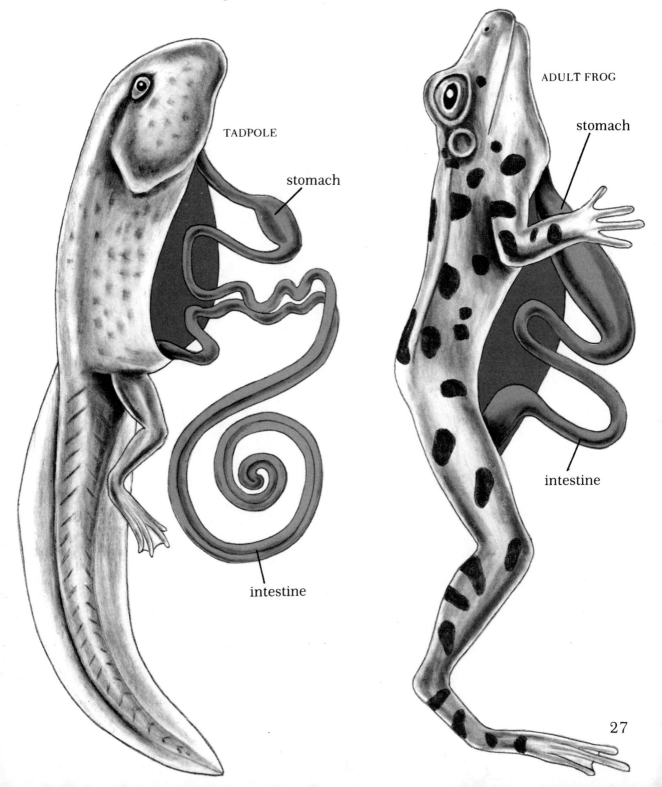

TADPOLE

stomach

intestine

ADULT FROG

stomach

intestine

27

TURTLE

The backbone and ribs of the turtle are joined to the inside of the shell.

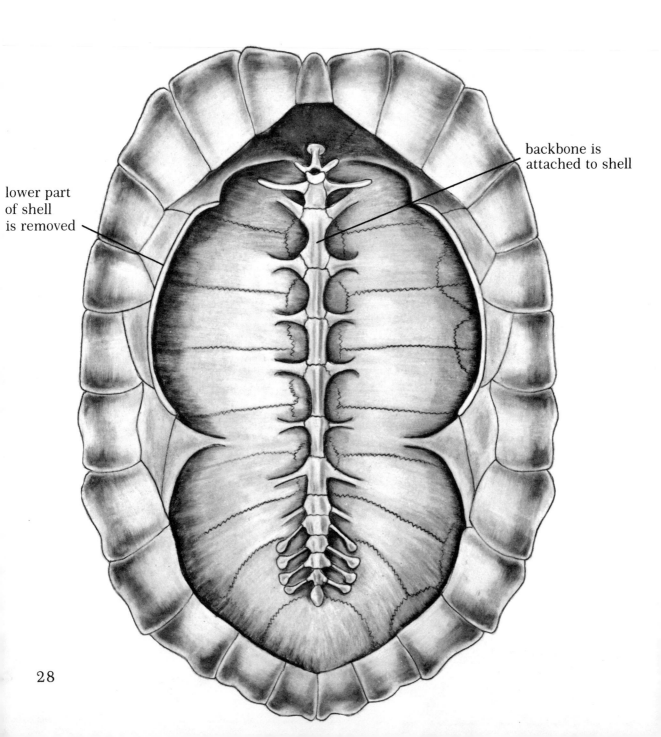

backbone is
attached to shell

lower part
of shell
is removed

The shell of the turtle protects its internal organs.

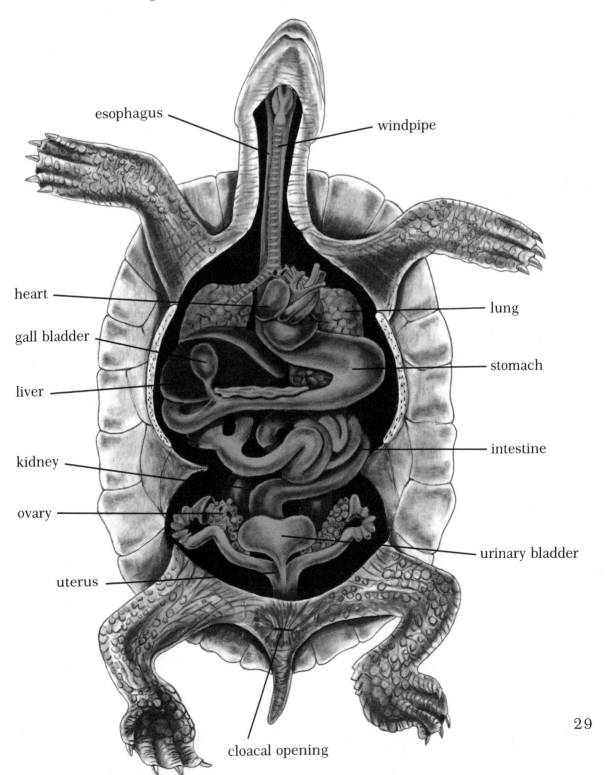

esophagus

windpipe

heart

lung

gall bladder

stomach

liver

kidney

intestine

ovary

urinary bladder

uterus

cloacal opening

SNAKE

All the snake's organs fit into a long thin body like the earthworm's. Unlike the earthworm, the snake is either male or female, and has a skeleton. The skeleton has ribs all the way from the head to the tail.

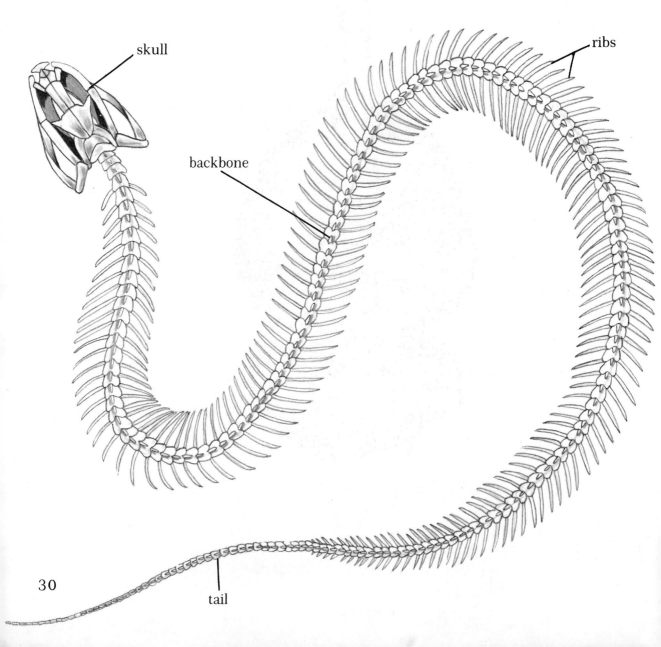

skull

ribs

backbone

tail

There is room for only one complete lung
in a long thin animal like the snake.

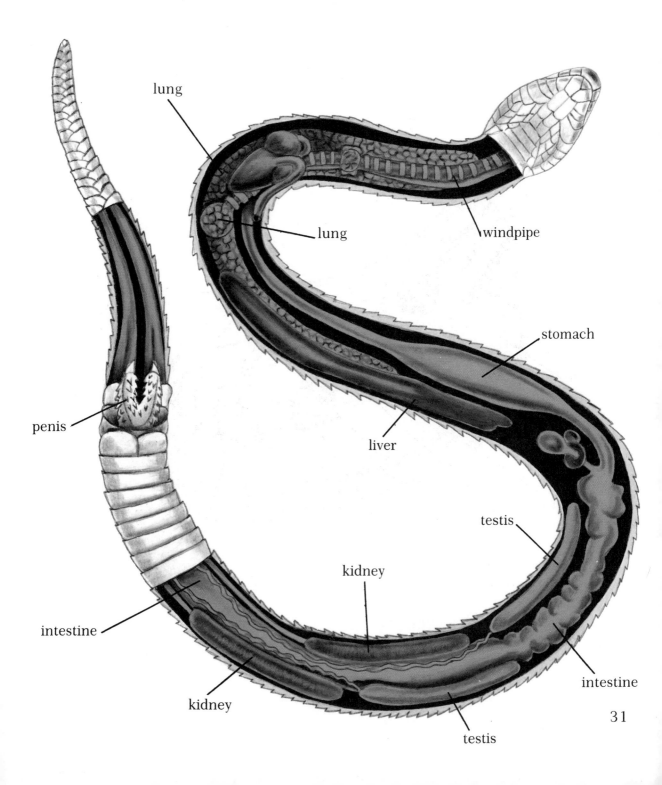

lung

lung

windpipe

stomach

liver

penis

testis

kidney

intestine

kidney

intestine

testis

31

BIRD

The body of a bird is built for flying. The bones are very light, and the muscles that move the wings are very large and strong.

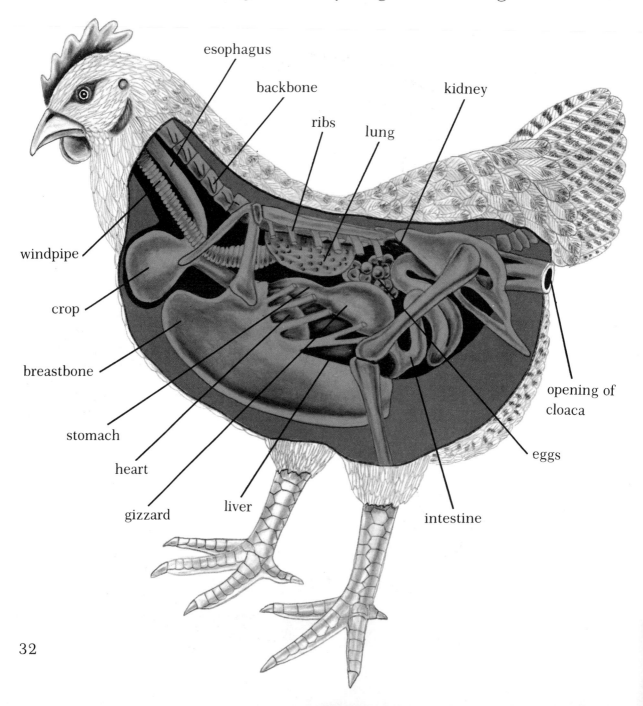

esophagus

backbone

kidney

ribs

lung

windpipe

crop

breastbone

stomach

heart

gizzard

liver

intestine

opening of cloaca

eggs

The shell of an egg hardens just before it is laid, when it passes through the birth canal.

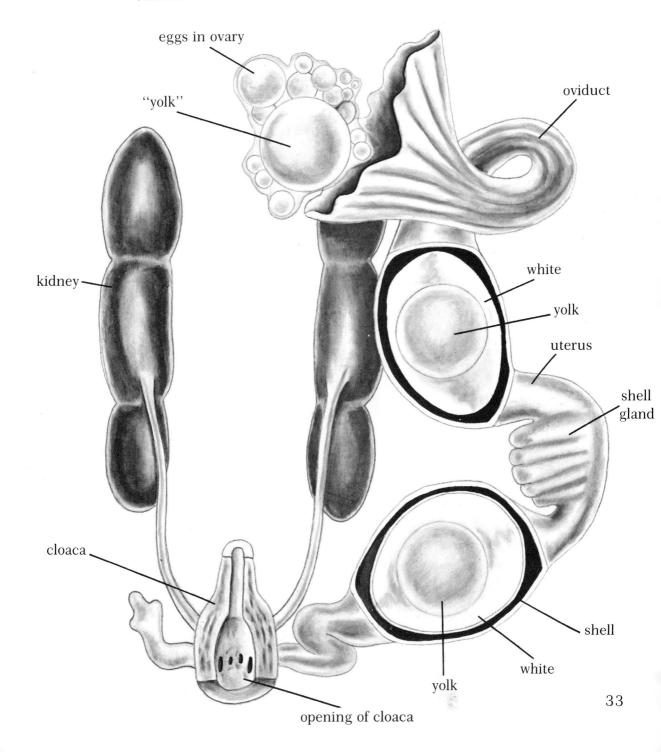

eggs in ovary

"yolk"

oviduct

kidney

white

yolk

uterus

shell gland

cloaca

shell

white

yolk

opening of cloaca

33

Bird's Egg

If we look inside a fertilized egg when a baby bird is starting to develop, we can see it growing on top of the yolk. The yolk is the food of the baby bird. The baby absorbs the food through blood vessels that travel from the yolk into its body.

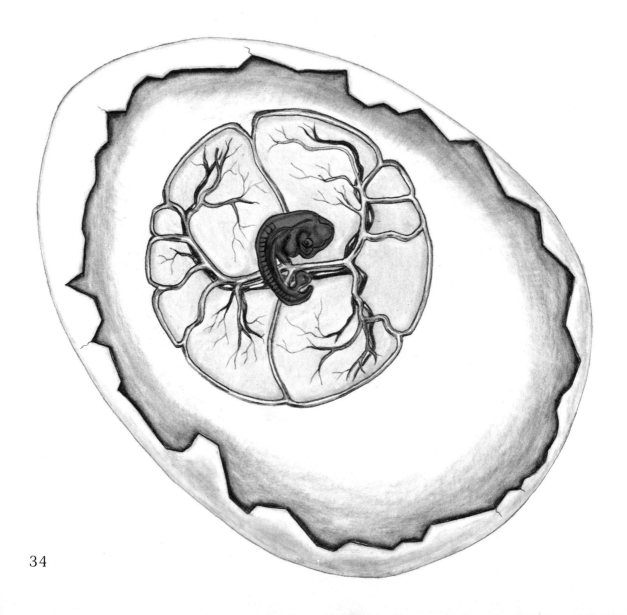

When the yolk has been used up, and the baby bird has grown so big that it is folded tightly inside the eggshell, the egg is ready to hatch.

GUINEA PIG

Guinea pigs are friendly and easy to care for. They make very good pets.

There are three main types of guinea pigs.

LONG-HAIRED, OR
PERUVIAN, GUINEA PIG

ROUGH-HAIRED, OR
ABYSSINIAN, GUINEA PIG

SMOOTH-HAIRED, OR
ENGLISH, GUINEA PIG

Underside of a Guinea Pig

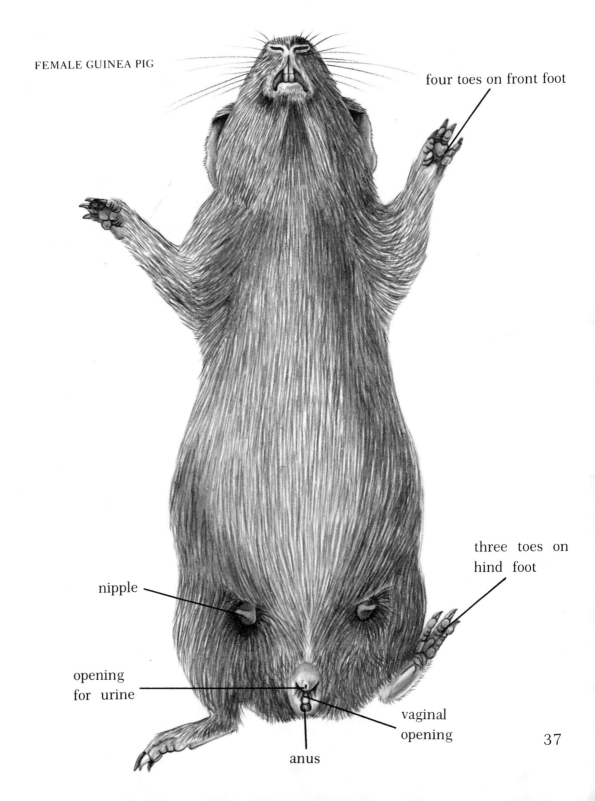

FEMALE GUINEA PIG

four toes on front foot

three toes on hind foot

nipple

opening
for urine

vaginal
opening

anus

37

Muscles of a Guinea Pig

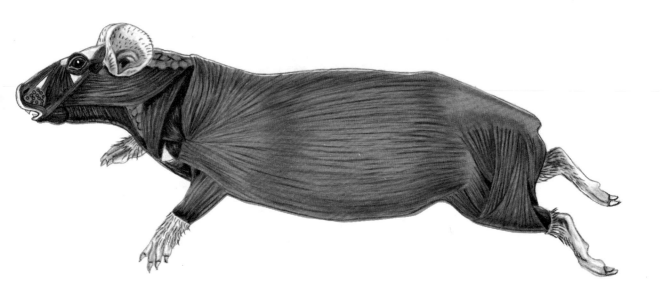

Skeleton of a Guinea Pig

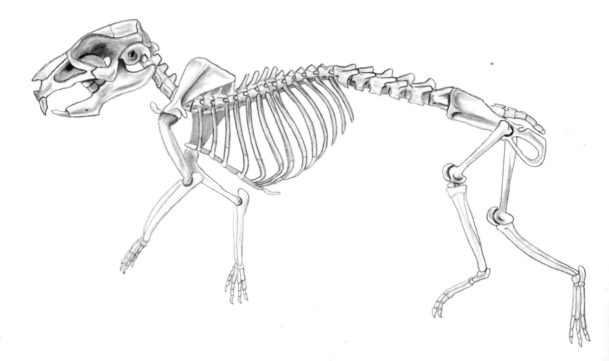

Organs of a Female Guinea Pig

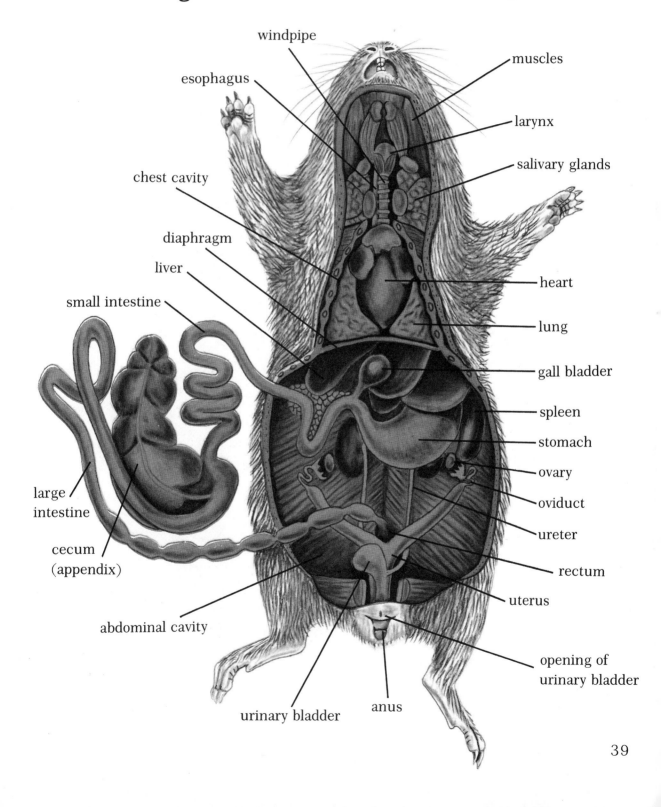

windpipe

muscles

esophagus

larynx

salivary glands

chest cavity

diaphragm

liver

heart

small intestine

lung

gall bladder

spleen

stomach

large intestine

ovary

oviduct

cecum (appendix)

ureter

rectum

uterus

abdominal cavity

opening of urinary bladder

urinary bladder

anus

Organs of a Male Guinea Pig

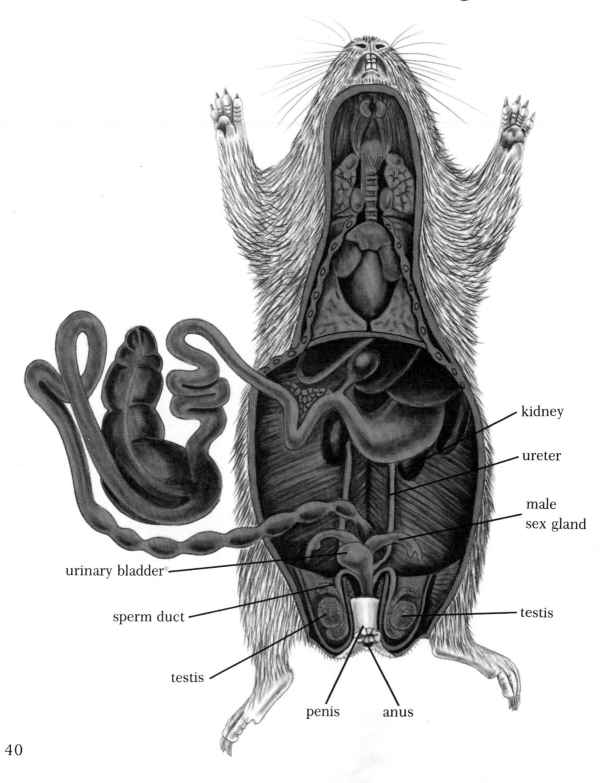

kidney

ureter

male
sex gland

urinary bladder

sperm duct

testis

testis

penis   anus

Pregnant Guinea Pig

Inside a Pregnant Guinea Pig

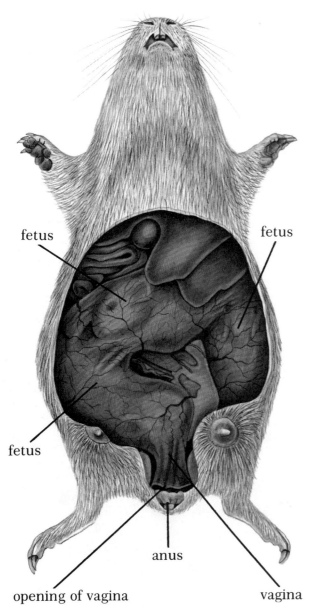

fetus

fetus

fetus

anus

opening of vagina

vagina

Baby Guinea Pig before Being Born

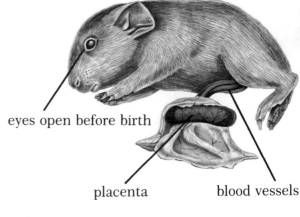

eyes open before birth

placenta

blood vessels

SPECIAL PARTS OF SPECIAL ANIMALS

Mouth of a Right Whale

Even though the right whale is huge, it eats tiny sea creatures called crustaceans. Inside the whale's mouth there are strainers called baleen plates. The whale eats by sucking in mouthfuls of water, straining out the food through the baleen plates, and then squeezing the water out of its mouth.

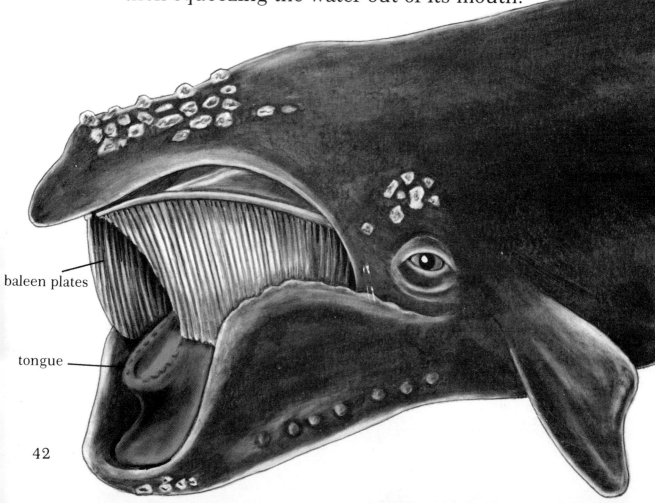

baleen plates

tongue

Poison Gland of a Snake

The fang of a rattlesnake injects its poison the way a doctor's syringe injects medicine. The fang, or tooth, is hollow and has a poison gland at its top. When the snake bites, tiny muscles squeeze poison from the gland down through the fang and into its prey.

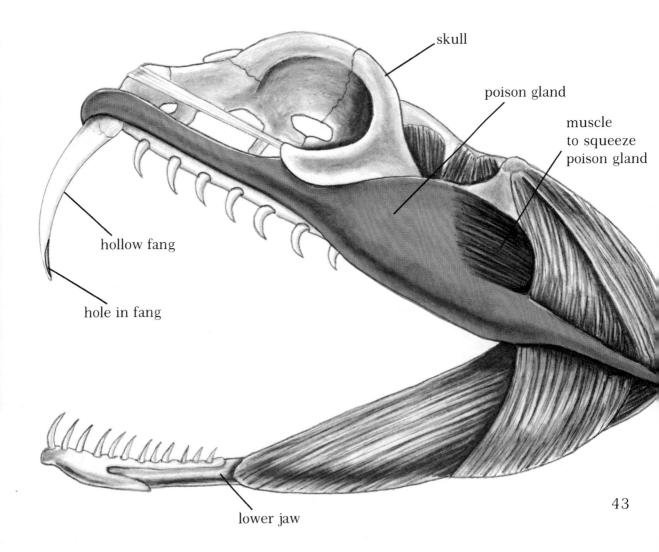

skull

poison gland

muscle to squeeze poison gland

hollow fang

hole in fang

lower jaw

43

Pouch of a Father Sea Horse

Father sea horses take care of their babies. They carry them in a special pouch. Each baby gets its nourishment from a yolk-filled sac attached to its own belly.

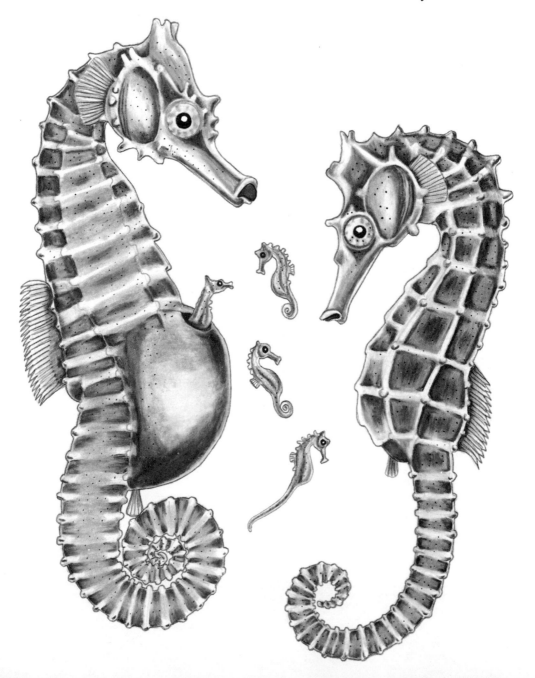

Shell of a Snail

Did you ever wonder why a snail doesn't lose its shell? It is very firmly attached—like this.

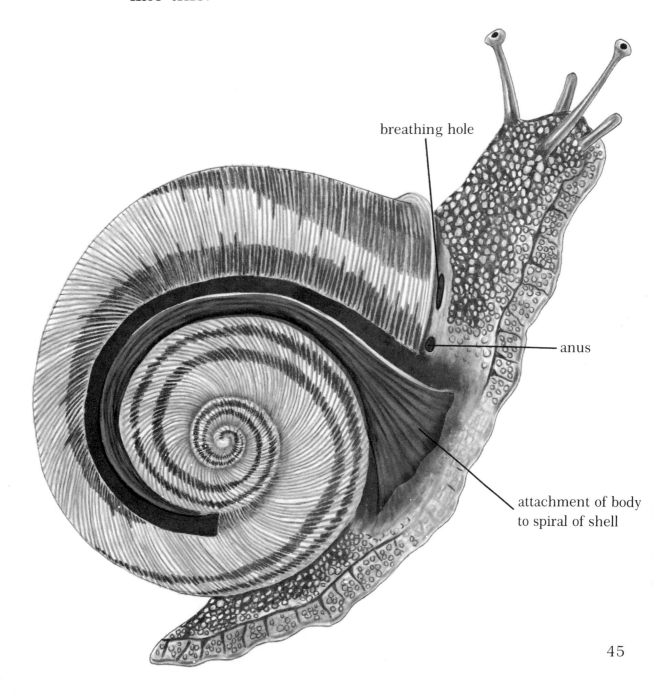

breathing hole

anus

attachment of body to spiral of shell

Neck of a Giraffe

Even though the giraffe has a long neck, it has no more vertebrae than other animals.

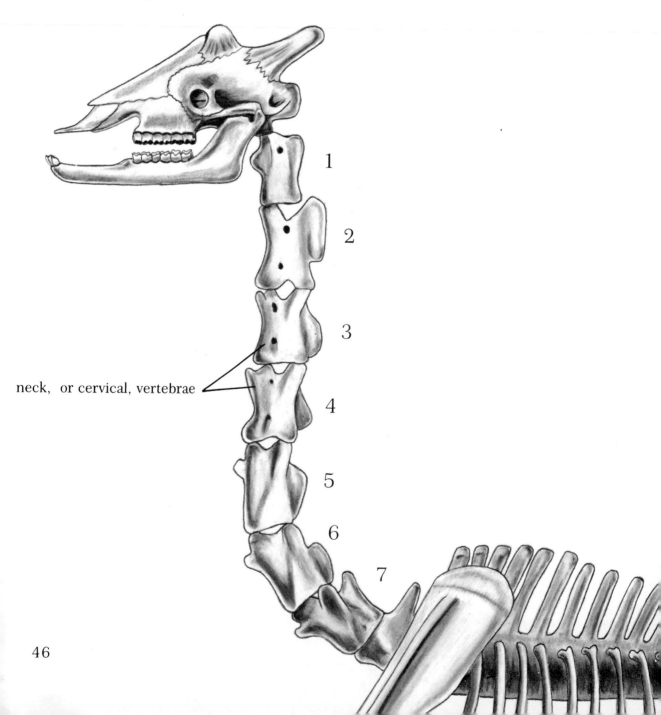

1

2

3

neck, or cervical, vertebrae

4

5

6

7

Silk Gland of a Spider

The spider has glands that make liquid silk. When the liquid is squeezed through spinnerets it becomes a delicate thread which the spider can form into a web.

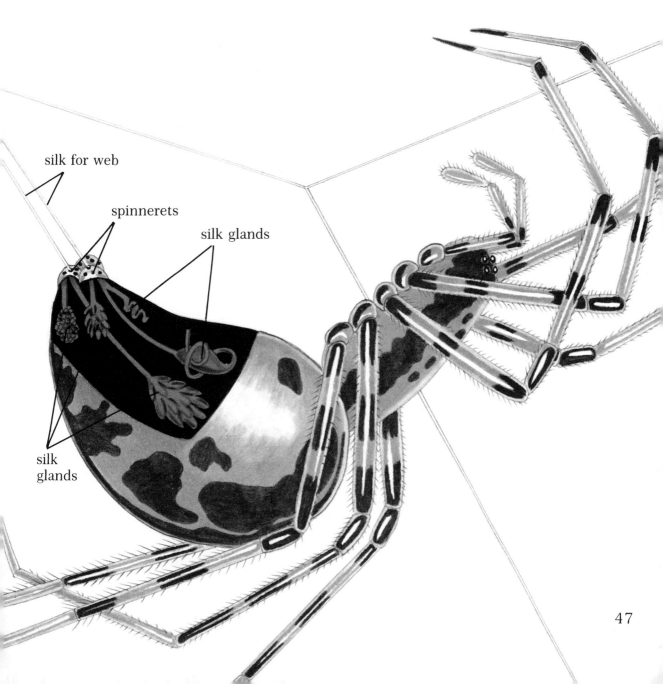

silk for web

spinnerets

silk glands

silk glands

Tongue of a Butterfly

The butterfly has a small head and no neck, but it drinks nectar from deep flowers. Its long tongue reaches to the bottom of blossoms.

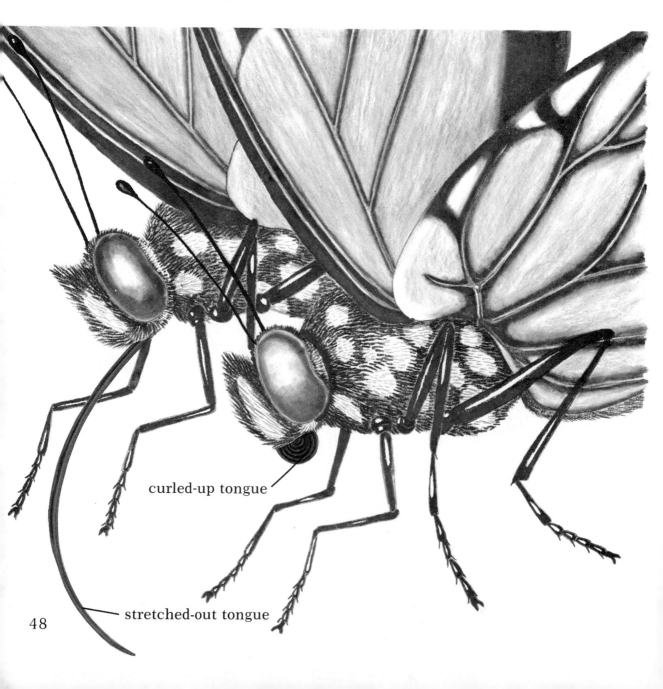

curled-up tongue

48   stretched-out tongue

Inside a Camel's Hump

A camel can live a long time on the desert without food. The hump consists of fat which the camel uses up when it is unable to get food.

The camel does not store water in its hump. It drinks very large amounts of water when it has a chance. When it can't drink, it gets water from desert plants.

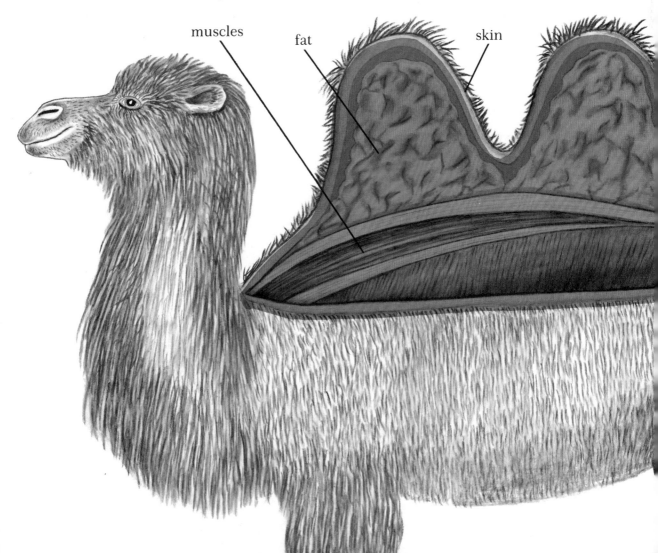

muscles   fat   skin

Tip of an Elephant's Trunk

If we look into the end of an elephant's trunk, we can see that it serves as both nose and hand. The Indian elephant has a movable fingerlike structure at the opening of its trunk. It can delicately pick up objects or food. The African elephant has two fingerlike projections. Both elephants have two nostrils which run all the way up the muscular trunk.

Mouth of a Mosquito

Not only does the female mosquito suck blood with her mouth, but she also injects a tiny bit of her saliva. The saliva makes the bite itch.

Stomachs of a Cow

The cow has four stomachs. When the cow eats, it swallows into stomach number one, then spits up the food to chew it some more. This food is called the cud. When the cow finishes chewing its cud, it swallows it into stomach number two. The food then goes to stomachs three and four, where more digestion takes place.

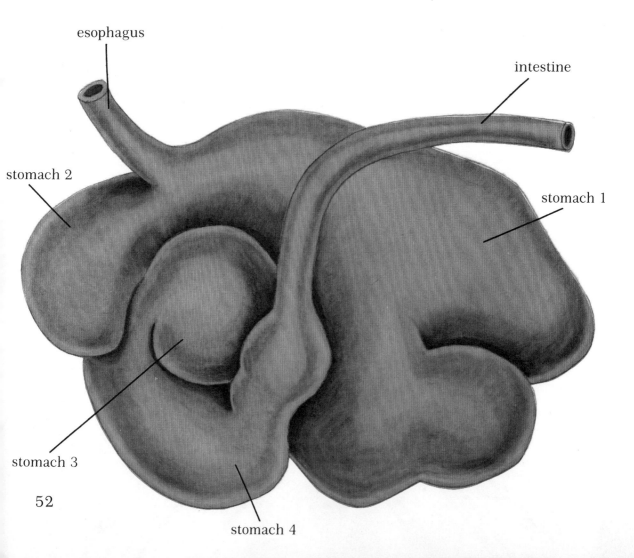

esophagus

intestine

stomach 2

stomach 1

stomach 3

52

stomach 4

Ink Sac of a Squid

When a squid wants protection, it squirts ink into the water so predators cannot see it.

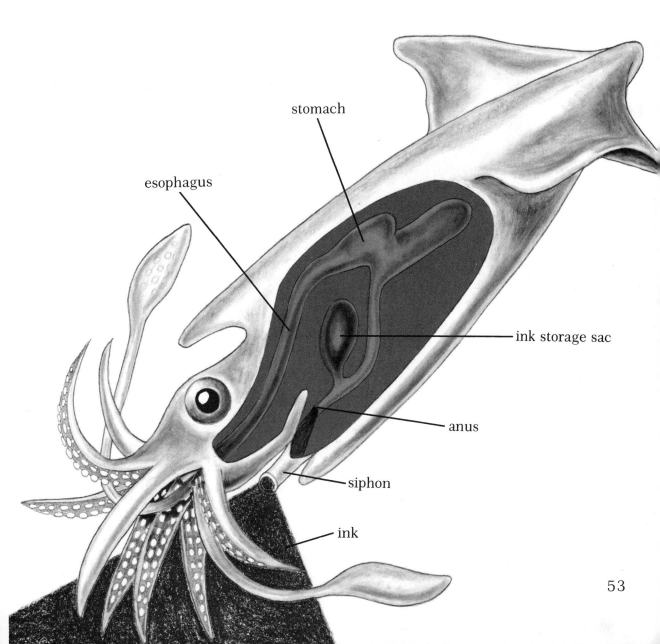

stomach

esophagus

ink storage sac

anus

siphon

ink

Mouth of a Jellyfish

A jellyfish has a funnel-shaped mouth in the middle of its body. The tentacles, which hang from the body, sting and entangle animals.

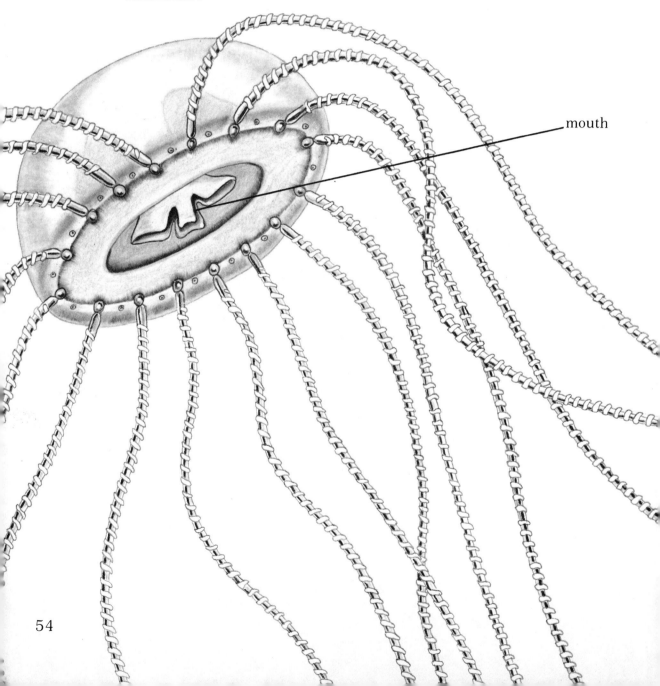

mouth

Ear of a Toad

Toads have ears. On each side of the toad's head there is a big round eardrum. Inside the eardrum a tiny earbone transmits sound waves to special nerves which carry messages to the brain.

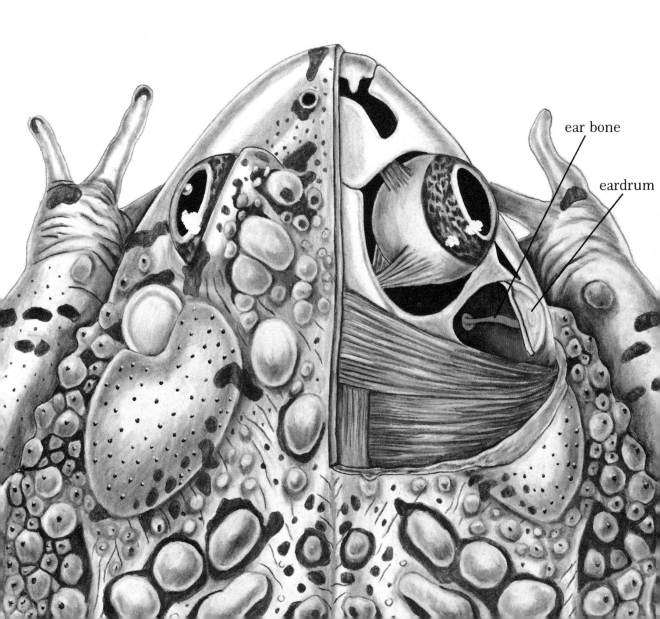

ear bone

eardrum

Flipper of a Seal

On the outside a seal's flipper looks like a paddle but on the inside there are five rows of bones. This is how we know that the ancient ancestor of seals had separate toes and probably walked on land.

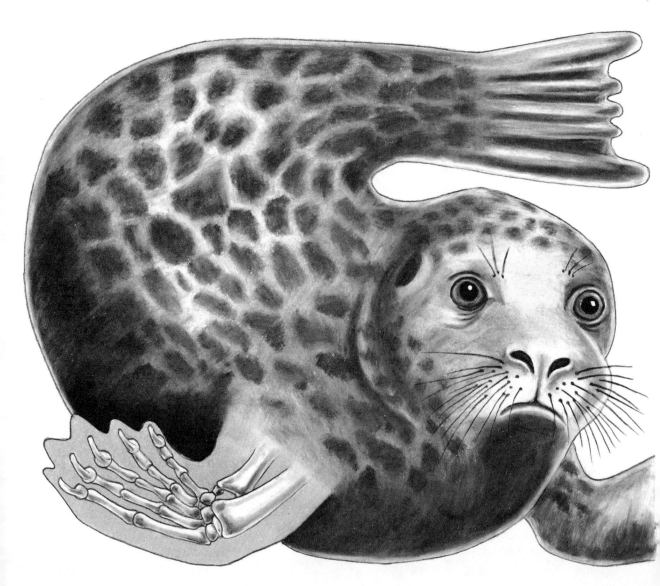

Wing of a Bird

By looking inside the wing of a bird we can see that the long feathers which a bird uses for flying are supported by the wing bones.

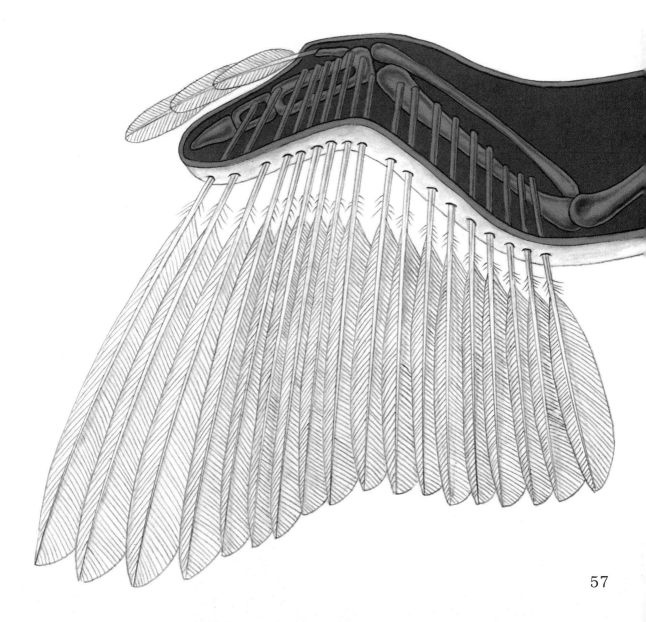

Mouth of a Hippopotamus

Hippopotamuses have huge mouths. They use their powerful teeth for pulling up and chewing water plants.

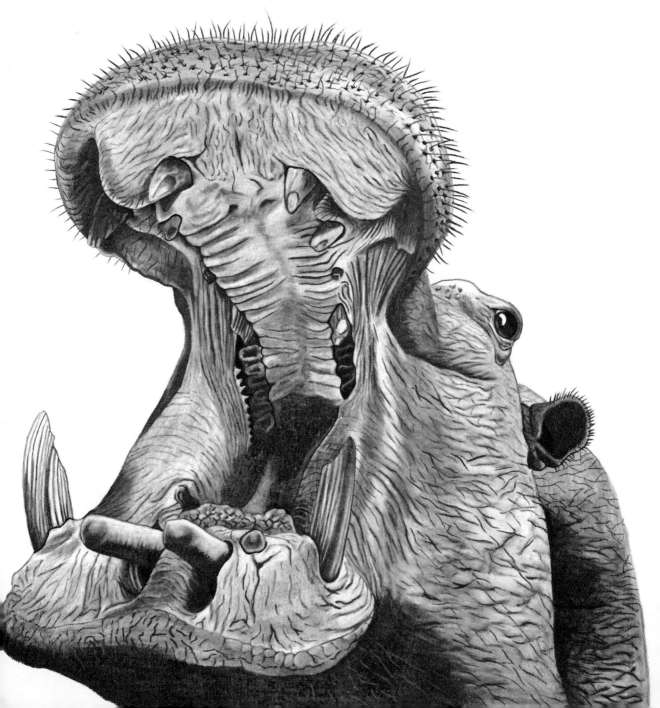

Shell of a Ladybug

The shell of a ladybug is really hardened wings. When the ladybug flies, these protective covers are lifted, and the bigger but delicate flying wings are unfurled.

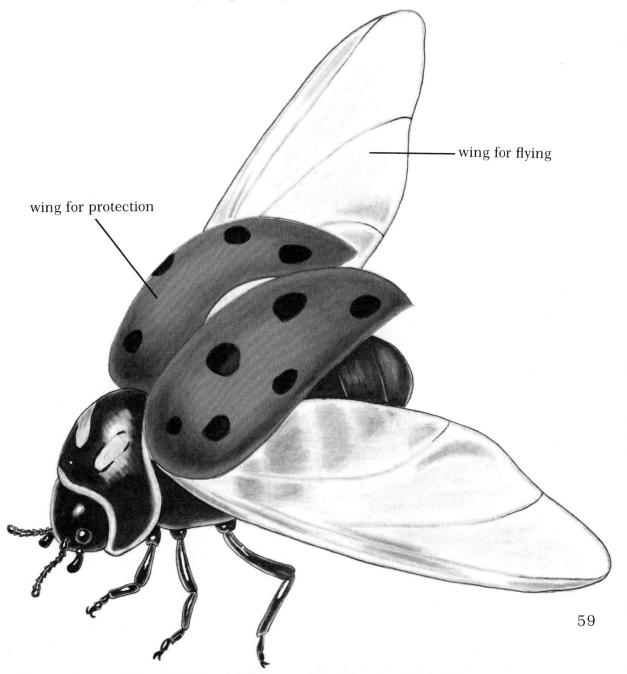

wing for flying

wing for protection

Sting of a Bee

If you have ever been stung by a bee you know that the sting gets left in the wound. Since the bee's sting is attached to other important organs, the bee dies of internal injuries after stinging. Here is how the sting is attached inside the bee.

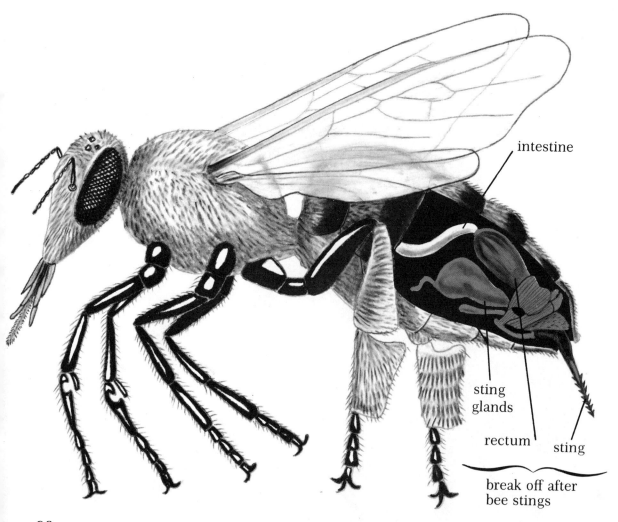

intestine

sting glands

rectum

sting

break off after bee stings

Pouch of a Kangaroo

The baby kangaroo spends much time during its two-year childhood inside its mother's pouch. This is how the inside of the pouch looks.

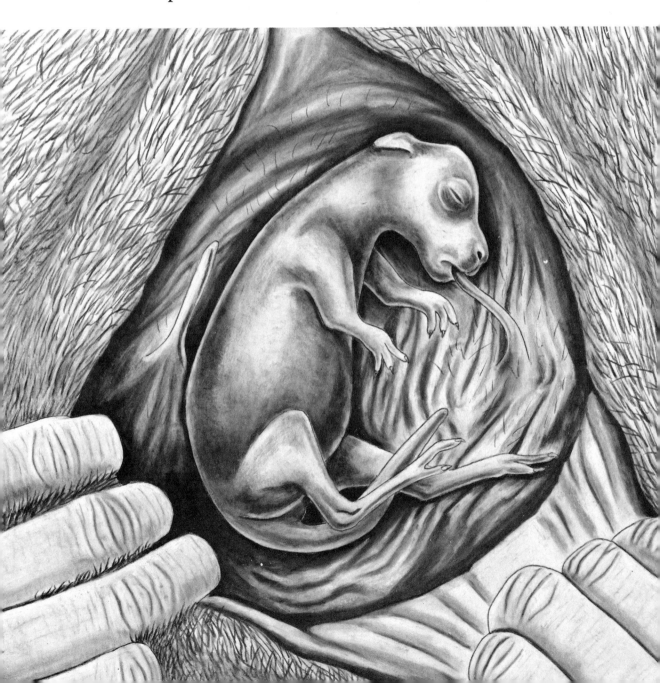

By looking closely and by looking inside many different animals, we can realize that all have specialized parts to best help them carry on their life functions. We can also now understand that even though they may look very different from one another, all animals have parts for eating, getting rid of wastes, breathing, and reproducing.

INDEX